NEW CRAFTS

STRINGWORK

NEW CRAFTS
STRINGWORK

DEENA BEVERLEY

PHOTOGRAPHY BY PETER WILLIAMS

LORENZ BOOKS
NEW YORK • LONDON • SYDNEY • BATH

This edition published in 1997 by Lorenz Books
27 West 20th Street, New York, New York 10011

LORENZ BOOKS are available for bulk purchase
for sales promotion and for premium use. For
details, write or call the manager of special
sales: Lorenz Books, 27 West 20th Street,
New York, New York 10011; (212) 807-6739

© 1997 Anness Publishing Limited

Lorenz Books is an imprint of
Anness Publishing Limited

ISBN 1 85967 377 5

Publisher: Joanna Lorenz
Senior editor: Clare Nicholson
Photographer: Peter Williams
Designer: Caroline Reeves
Stylist: Deena Beverley
Illustrator: Vana Haggerty

Printed and bound in Hong Kong

10 9 8 7 6 5 4 3 2 1

CONTENTS

INTRODUCTION

THE DECORATIVE USE OF STRING AND ROPE HAS ENJOYED A RENAISSANCE IN RECENT YEARS. WHETHER THEY ARE WRAPPED SIMPLY AROUND RUSTIC-STYLE CANDLE HOLDERS, OR WORKED INTO THE ELABORATE TRIMMINGS KNOWN AS PASSEMENTERIE, STRING AND ROPE HAVE REGAINED PROMINENCE AS FAVORED MATERIALS OF DESIGNERS AND ARTISTS AROUND THE WORLD.

STRING AND ROPE CAN BE FOUND AT MANY KINDS OF STORES. BESIDES OBVIOUS SOURCES — SUCH AS HIGH-END HARDWARE STORES AND DEPARTMENT STORES — EVEN THE MOST SEEMINGLY INCONGRUOUS OUTLETS ARE LIKELY TO HAVE A SUPPLY OF SOME TYPE OF ROPE OR STRING. IT IS THIS UNIVERSAL ACCESSIBILITY, AS WELL AS THE LOW COST OF THE RAW MATERIALS, THAT HELP ACCESSIBILITY AND LOW COST TO MAKE STRING AND ROPE SUCH APPEALING MEDIA WITH WHICH TO WORK.

Left: The diversity of the colors and textures of string materials allows scope for creating wonderful objects. The balls and spools of string are also decorative in their own right.

STRING AND ROPE — A TRADITIONAL CRAFT

FROM SIMPLE, HANDMADE, TWO-STRAND TWISTS TO COMPLEX MACHINE-MADE ROPES BUILT AROUND A STURDY CORE, STRING AND ROPE HAVE BEEN KEPT AND USED IN ALMOST EVERY HOME IN THE WORLD. THEY HAVE BEEN FASHIONED INTO AN AMAZINGLY DIVERSE RANGE OF PRACTICAL AND DECORATIVE ITEMS, INCLUDING BANISTER ROPES IN GRAND HOUSES, THATCH-TYING MATERIALS ON CROFTERS' COTTAGES, AS WELL AS STRAPS, BELTS, SLINGS AND BASKETS IN PRIMITIVE CULTURES.

Ropework is one of the oldest folk arts. Initially seized upon and perfected by sailors, almost every walk of life has borrowed from the art. Anglers, farmers, butchers, cooks, firemen, florists, gardeners, homemakers, upholsterers, bookbinders, boy and girl scouts, hot-air balloonists and even tree surgeons all produce knots peculiar to their tasks.

As with all folk arts, necessity bred invention, with the available materials determining the crafts that were practiced. A multitude of fibers – vegetable, animal and synthetic – have been twisted together to produce strong rope formations in almost every culture. Naval seamen have traditionally specialized in the technique of square knotting (macramé), as only log line, fishing line and other thin materials were available in sufficient quantities for practice work. Merchant sailors were generally better supplied and, although they were seldom issued with new rope, the range of discarded materials they could use was more varied, resulting in heavier, ornate work known as decorative marlin-spike seamanship (applied knots).

The interest of seamen in their knots was widespread, intense and often fiercely competitive. Complex knots were explained under pledge of secrecy, and knowledge of one knot was often bartered for that of another. Superlative knot-makers were very highly regarded. A great many small items were required on board ship; these were produced by the

sailors on board, and included everything from handles for chests, doors, buckets and drawers to fastenings on laundry and ditty bags (small bags that the sailors used to hold needles and thread).

Indeed, one of the earliest volumes devoted to the subject – *The Book of Knots*, published by Hodge and Chamier in 1866 – appeared under the nautical-sounding pseudonym "Tom Bowling" to impress its sea-loving readers.

Above: String and rope have always been widely used in nautical applications. Sailors traditionally have great skill with and knowledge of knots and ropecraft.

The undisputed king of knots is Clifford W. Ashley, although he ascribes an authoritative status to Darcy Lever, author of *Sheet Anchor* (1808). *The Ashley Book of Knots* was truly a life's work, comprising instructions for over 4000 knots.

Above: The wildly contrasting repair on this synthetic net bag emphasizes the workaday nature of nautical knotting. Whatever materials are on hand are used.

Left: Fenders on ships are made in a wide range of knots. They are designed to prevent the paintwork from being scuffed as the ship enters port; similarly elaborate knot formations appear on floats.

Only knots that were functional in nature were included in Ashley's book, but throughout history decorative knots, which would in reality be impractical, have been featured as a motif in art. Such knots appear on tombstones, early book covers, ancient architectural carvings and in illuminated manuscripts. Knots were used in many heraldic devices, and artists such as Leonardo da Vinci have drawn elaborate knot forms in their work. Patterns have also been created by pressing rope into the surface of wet clay to produce an imprint, and by the ever-popular decorative technique of using twisted ropes of china clay to embellish simple pots and fine porcelain alike.

Knotting formed the basis of string and rope crafts from the ninth century on, but contemporary work features many other techniques, some utilizing little more than a simple wrapping of string or rope. Christian Astuguevielle has made rope-wrapping into an art form, and the rope-wrapped chair shown in this book is a homage to his work. (The string-wrapped tumblers and the string-wrapped candelabra are less-demanding versions of this technique.)

Whether looped loosely around a muslin curtain as a delightfully simple tieback, or worked into fantastically complex knots and tassels for more elaborate tastes, these inexpensive and universally available materials have something to offer everyone.

Above: Twisted and knotted rope forms a sturdy handle for this urn.

GALLERY

S TRING IS AN EXTREMELY VERSATILE MEDIUM THAT HAS BEEN USED IN CRAFTWORK FOR MANY YEARS. PRESENTED HERE IS A SELECTION OF THE WIDE RANGE OF OBJECTS THAT CAN BE MADE USING STRING OR ROPE.

ONCE YOU HAVE PRACTICED THE BASIC TECHNIQUES AND WORKED ON SOME OF THE PROJECTS IN THE FOLLOWING PAGES, THESE GALLERY ITEMS WILL PROVIDE EVEN MORE PRACTICAL AND INSPIRATIONAL IDEAS.

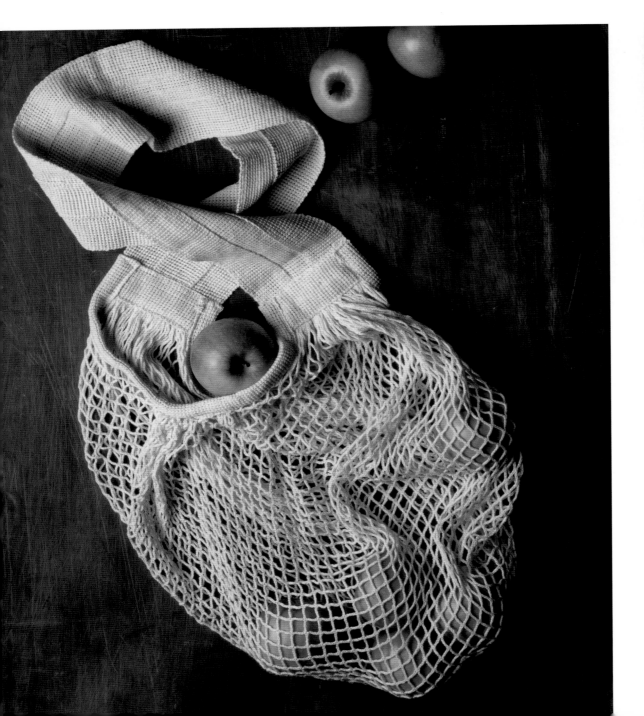

Left: The string bag is a design classic. It is lightweight, can be packed away to nothing when not in use, and allows ventilation of fruit and vegetables when in transit.

Above: Earthy terracotta is offset by smooth, white rope in a practical wine cooler that will withstand years of use.

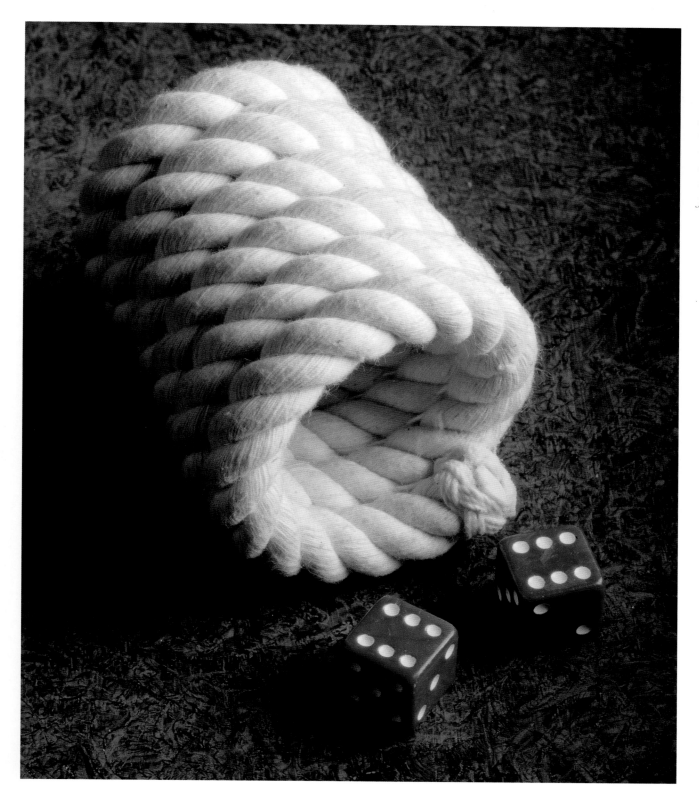

Left: When making household objects, the method of coiling rope is most often associated with placemats. This dice cup is another use of this simple method, creating an attractive yet functional object.

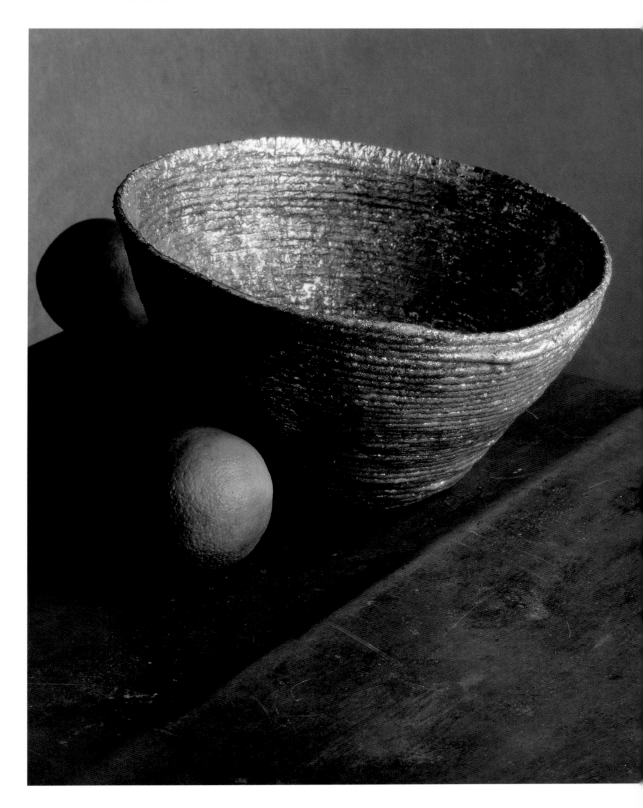

Above: Some macramé pieces are of such simple design that they are timeless. This child's chair would look adorable hanging from a sturdy tree in the garden.

Right: Cotton string loses its utilitarian image when glamorized with a verdigris paint effect and gilded in metal leaf.

Opposite: Those practicing the passementerie's art are constantly finding new and exciting materials that reflect trends in interior design. Smooth metal contrasts beautifully with rough jute in this elegant group of tassels.

Above: String can also be used as an art material. This cowboy is appliquéd using string to give a wonderful collage effect.

Left: Beauty rests in utility, as this simple wooden string holder, holding a satisfyingly large ball of garden twine, proves admirably.

Far left: This wonderfully decorative bell knocker has been elaborately knotted and finished with a Turk's Head knot.

Left: A simple wrapping of green garden twine adds rustic charm to a plain candlestick.

MATERIALS

STRING AND ROPE ARE AVAILABLE IN A WONDERFUL ARRAY OF SIZES, COLORS AND MATERIALS, BOTH NATURAL AND ARTIFICIAL. THROUGHOUT HISTORY THEY HAVE BEEN MADE FROM WHATEVER HAS BEEN AVAILABLE, INCLUDING NETTLES, HEMP AND BLACKBERRY STALKS. MANY OF THE PROJECTS IN THIS BOOK USE UNUSUAL MATERIALS THAT GIVE STRIKING RESULTS, SUCH AS RAFFIA, PAPER ROPE AND PIPING CORD. CHOOSE ACCORDING TO THE EFFECT YOU WISH TO ACHIEVE: SMOOTH FOR AN ELEGANT FINISH, OR TEXTURED FOR RUSTIC APPEAL.

Plasterer's jute scrim is an open woven mesh used to make seams. The plaster is forced through the holes to adhere smoothly, creating a firm bond. In string crafts, scrim is a decorative material forming attractive fringes and netting.

Polyester rope is suitable for heavy-duty use, as it is very strong. Available in a variety of thicknesses and colors, it will give a contemporary, urban feel to many of the projects in this book. For instance, by substituting a vivid polyester rope for the natural sash cord used for the deck chair, and painting the wooden frame a bright color, an entirely different look could be achieved. Polyester rope is available at hardware stores, as well as at outlets stocking ship chandlery and climbing equipment.

Sisal rope and string are made from the prepared fiber of the agave and fourcroya plants. They are very strong and pleasingly textural.

Coir rope is made from coconut husks. It is strong and, as you would expect, hairy. It is perfect for projects in which a naive, "rough-and-ready" finish is required.

Sash cord is available in both waxed and unwaxed forms at hardware stores. It is made from different materials, including jute and polypropylene, and in several colors, including white, natural and white with red flecks. Sash cord is strong enough to bear the weight of heavy windows, and it is ideal for applications requiring a durable finish, such as the deck chair. The wide bore of this cord makes it easy to work with, and it produces a chunky, substantial-looking finish.

Piping cord, widely available at department and notions stores, is firm and flexible. It comes in several different thicknesses.

Cotton rope is soft, malleable and wonderfully easy to work with, yet has a durable, strong finish. It holds three-dimensional shapes well, such as in the Woven Stool Seat project. It is available at hardware stores.

Cotton string is flexible and of delicate coloring, making it perfect for projects requiring a subtle, tensile quality, such as the String-trimmed Bag.

Flax rope, made from flax fiber, is incredibly durable. Pieces of flax linen have been found in the pyramids of Egypt in remarkably sound condition.

Paper cord has become tremendously popular in floristry and gift-wrapping in recent years. Some varieties unravel to produce a wide ribbon that holds three-dimensional shapes well while others are designed to be used purely as strong, decorative cord.

Jute string is made in both tarred and untarred forms. Tar gives a rich, dark sheen to the twine and renders it more weatherproof, so this type is perfect for garden applications; untarred string is better suited to most indoor craft projects. Both types of jute string are available at hardware and garden-supply stores.

Raffia is ideal for gift-wrapping and floristry work, and it is available at garden-supply stores, stationers and in bulk at specialty craft suppliers.

Garden twine is also available at hardware and garden-supply stores. It comes in many shades of green, as well as in its natural color.

KEY

1 Plasterer's jute scrim	**12** Flax rope
2 Polyester rope	**13** Piping cord
3 Sisal	**14** Paper cord
4 Sisal	**15** Jute string
5 Coir rope	**16** White cotton string
6 Red-flecked sash cord	**17** Raffia
7 Sash cord	**18** Green garden twine
8 Sash cord	**19** Green garden twine
9 Piping cord	**20** Brown garden twine
10 Cotton rope	
11 Cotton string	

EQUIPMENT

ONLY THE MOST BASIC TOOLS AND EQUIPMENT ARE REQUIRED TO PRODUCE ALL THE PROJECTS IN THIS BOOK, ALTHOUGH MORE SPECIALIZED EQUIPMENT — SUCH AS A ROTARY HOLE PUNCH AND A GLUE GUN — WILL MAKE LARGER-SCALE PROJECTS EASIER AND MORE PLEASANT TO DO. CHOOSING AND USING THE CORRECT EQUIPMENT WILL ENSURE NEAT AND PROFESSIONAL RESULTS. THE SINGLE MOST IMPORTANT TOOL IS, OF COURSE, YOUR HANDS: INDEED, MOST STRING- AND ROPEWORK HAS BEEN PRACTICED FOR CENTURIES USING NO ADDITIONAL EQUIPMENT WHATSOEVER.

Extra-strong white glue is an absolute dream for use in string crafts. It allows bonding of string, even to difficult vertical surfaces, with pinpoint accuracy, cleanliness and economy.

Instant bonding (cyano-acrylate) glue is superb for dripping onto string to prevent ends from unraveling.

Spray adhesive is useful for delicate work that would be disturbed by a brush application of glue, although any "over-spray" can be messy and difficult to clean up. Only use when it is not possible to glue by other methods.

Glue gun and glue sticks are ideal for heavy-duty applications, particularly those requiring adhesion to vertical or curved surfaces. An instant bond is easily formed, although excess strands of glue can be tedious to remove. Be careful not to burn your hands on the hot glue.

Adhesive applicators Wooden tongue depressors and wooden skewers are perfect for applying glue.

Measuring equipment Accuracy in measuring will ensure professional results. A soft pencil, set square and metal ruler are all essential tools.

Cutting equipment A craft knife, scalpel and scissors will be sufficient to make all the projects in this book. For safety and accuracy, always use a clean, sharp blade in the knife and scalpel. A cutting mat, while not essential, will protect your work surface, aid accuracy and preserve the life of a blade. Alternatively, work on a pile of magazines.

Painting equipment In addition to a range of paintbrushes, a small sponge roller (used with a paint tray) will be useful for string painting, and some wood scraps will make handy stamping blocks. Latex, acrylic and gouache paints have been used for projects throughout. Choose paint that is right for the job—for example, fast-drying stamping paint (available at stationers and art supply stores) will make the gift-wrap project clean and quick to do. A paint palette is useful if you are working with small quantities of several different colors. Always have a jar of water in which to clean your brush if you are using water-based paints. If you are painting with oils, clean the brushes in turpentine immediately after use.

Wood filler, with a spatula for mixing and a palette knife for easy application, can be used to fill gaps and to smooth surfaces. The surface can then be smoothed even more with steel wool or a sanding block once dry.

Fabric stiffener is easy to apply, and it gives fabric and string additional body stiffness. It is also used when covering molds, as in the Food Cover.

Hammer and awl A hammer and awl are useful for driving rope securely into place when it has been so tightly woven that it becomes taut and difficult to work.

Rotary hole punch This is useful as a tool for making holes of various sizes, and it will add a smooth, professional finish to many of the projects in this book.

Cordless drill/screwdriver If you are planning to work on several projects, a cordless drill or screwdriver will be a sound investment. Choose a drill or screwdriver that can also be used manually.

Needles and bodkins For thicker cords the glue-dripping method will not provide a sufficiently fine point to the string for it to be threaded through a needle, so a bodkin, which is a curved needle with a larger eye, will be required. A sewing needle is also needed for some of the basic stitching involved. Choose the correct-sized eye for the width of the string or thread.

Beads will add glamour and textural interest to string and rope projects. Choose carefully for a sophisticated, understated result.

Pins and clips Clothespins and metal clips are very useful for holding string or rope in place as it dries, particularly on more challenging wrapping projects such as the chair. Although the adhesives recommended throughout will form fast, secure bonds, clamping a piece of work in place as the glue sets will ensure ease of working and consistent, neat results. Clothespins are also helpful for holding string in position at a safe distance from your fingers as instant-bonding glue is dripped onto it for ease of threading.

Release agents When shaping string or rope around a mold, as in the Food Cover, use of the appropriate release agents (clear plastic wrap and petroleum jelly, in this case) will ensure that you can release the finished item smoothly from the mold.

Protective and clean-up equipment
When working with adhesives and paint, it is wise to protect your work surface from drips and splashes before you begin. Brown paper is better for this purpose than newspaper, as newsprint could transfer itself onto pale string or delicate papers. Masking tape can be used to cover specific areas before painting or using adhesive. Absorbent paper towels will be useful to mop up any spills. Protect your hands with disposable plastic gloves when working with adhesive.

KEY
1 Extra-strong white glue
2 Spray adhesive
3 Glue gun and glue sticks
4 Tongue depressors and wooden skewers
5 Soft pencil
6 Metal ruler and set square
7 Scalpel
8 Craft knife
9 Scissors
10 Cutting mat
11 Paintbrushes
12 Small sponge roller and paint tray
13 Fast-drying stamp paints
14 Paint palette
15 Wood filler, with spatula
16 Palette knife
17 Steel wool
18 Sanding block
19 Fabric stiffener
20 Hammer
21 Rotary hole punch
22 Cordless drill/screwdriver and attachments
23 Needles
24 Large bodkins
25 Clothespins and metal clips
26 Petroleum jelly
27 Clear plastic wrap
28 Disposable plastic gloves
29 Brown paper and other papers
30 Masking tape
31 Water
32 Absorbent paper towels

BASIC TECHNIQUES

Sᴛʀɪɴɢ ᴀɴᴅ ʀᴏᴘᴇ ᴀʀᴇ ᴀᴍᴀᴢɪɴɢʟʏ ᴠᴇʀsᴀᴛɪʟᴇ ᴍᴇᴅɪᴀ — ᴛʜᴇʏ ᴍᴀʏ ʙᴇ ʙʀᴀɪᴅᴇᴅ, ᴄᴏɪʟᴇᴅ, ᴡᴏᴠᴇɴ, ᴡʀᴀᴘᴘᴇᴅ, ᴋɴᴏᴛᴛᴇᴅ, ᴀᴘᴘʟɪǫᴜᴇᴅ, ᴇᴍʙʀᴏɪᴅᴇʀᴇᴅ ᴀɴᴅ ᴇᴠᴇɴ ᴋɴɪᴛᴛᴇᴅ ɪɴᴛᴏ sɪᴍᴘʟᴇ ᴏʀ ᴄᴏᴍᴘʟᴇx ᴘᴀᴛᴛᴇʀɴs ꜰᴏʀ ᴘʀᴀᴄᴛɪᴄᴀʟ ᴏʀ ᴅᴇᴄᴏʀᴀᴛɪᴠᴇ ᴘᴜʀᴘᴏsᴇs. Iᴛ ɪs ǫᴜɪᴛᴇ ᴍᴀɢɪᴄᴀʟ ᴛʜᴀᴛ ᴡɪᴛʜ ᴊᴜsᴛ ᴀ ꜰᴇᴡ ʙᴀsɪᴄ ᴛᴇᴄʜɴɪǫᴜᴇs ᴀɴ ᴇssᴇɴᴛɪᴀʟʟʏ ᴏɴᴇ-ᴅɪᴍᴇɴsɪᴏɴᴀʟ ᴍᴀᴛᴇʀɪᴀʟ ᴄᴀɴ ᴀssᴜᴍᴇ ᴀʟᴍᴏsᴛ ᴀɴʏ ꜰᴏʀᴍ.

The enthusiastic stringworker can learn complex knots and embark upon fine embroidery and passementerie projects, but even a young child can tackle stringwork. Cat's cradle is a simple and popular game that introduces many children to the adaptability of string, not to mention jump ropes and tug-of-war. Simple knots are used by almost everyone in every walk of life, for decorative and practical purposes alike. Studying and practicing basic techniques will make the projects in this book even easier.

ESTIMATING YARN REQUIREMENTS
To establish how much string or rope is needed to complete a macramé project, multiply the required finished length by eight, then multiply this figure by half the number of strands to be used. This is a sum that sounds far more complex in theory than it is in practice.

THREADING STRING AND ROPE
Threading string and rope through holes and eyelets is a practical way of fastening, as in many nautical uses, but can also be purely decorative, as on the simple lampshade edging illustrated here, or to make an elegant hanging out of found objects.

It is possible to thread string onto a large needle, but this is not always necessary unless you actually plan to stitch with the string as though it were thread.

The raw end of the string or rope can be rendered much more rigid and less likely to fray, and correspondingly easier to thread, if it is treated with fast-drying glue before use.

Preparing the string or rope

1 Catch the end of the string or rope in a wooden clothespin. Wood is preferable to plastic, as it grips string and rope better, but is not essential.

2 Holding the string or rope between the finger and thumb of one hand, rotate the clothespin until the string or rope becomes tightly twisted but has not quite started to double back on itself.

3 Working over a protected surface, drip a few drops of instant-bonding glue onto the string, allowing it to saturate the short length that is held taut between finger and thumb and clothespin.

4 Let the glue dry thoroughly before snipping halfway through the glued part of the string or rope. The end is now narrow and firm enough to thread comfortably. This gluing technique can be used to seal the other end of the string or rope when the project is complete.

Whatever the project, make sure the hole through which the string or rope will be threaded is an appropriate size. This may sound like stating the obvious, but if the hole is too small, an uneven, strained look will result; if the hole is too large (for example, if a hole punch with only one, large setting is used), the finish will be ungainly.

Threading

1 Having taken care to match the width of the string to the size of the hole, pull the string through gently so as not to fray it unduly against the possibly rough interior edges of the punched hole. Brace your other hand against the material through which you are threading so that it does not become creased or distorted as the string is passed through it.

2 When most of the string has passed through the hole, take care to consider exactly how tightly it needs to be threaded for the best decorative effect. A gentle tension, leaving loops of even size, adds sophistication to this lampshade.

APPLIQUÉ WITH STRING AND ROPE

All kinds of delightful designs can be wrought by stitching simple swirls of string or rope onto fabrics. Choose a string or rope to complement or contrast with the base fabric. Here a soft, pure wool blanket with a floppy fringe becomes chic when appliquéd with a single strand pulled from a three-strand sisal rope packed with rough-and-ready texture.

1 Allow the string or rope to untwist onto the surface of the fabric. As you let it uncoil, it will naturally fall into twists and swirls, upon which it is difficult and unnecessary to improve.

2 If you are a beginner, you may like to safety pin the design in place before stitching. Ease the swirls into position without affecting the actual pattern, so the design is evenly spaced from the edge of the fabric.

3 Thread a needle with strong thread. Secure the thread on the surface of the fabric with a few stitches where it will be hidden when the string or rope has been appliquéd. Pick up a tiny piece of the fabric with the needle making sure it is along the line where the string or rope will lie.

4 Bring the needle up through the string or rope. Pull the thread taut.

5 Take the needle back through the string or rope, concealing the thread within its twists and working along the design. Continue to slip stitch the design in this way.

WHIPPING

This is a technique of binding together one or more lengths of rope using either twine or string. When finished, the ends are invisible and the finish is very strong and neat.

1 Take the end of a length of twine and form a loop leaving about 3 inches at one end. Position the loop against the string or rope where the binding is to begin.

2 Wrap the other end of the twine around both the rope and twine several times, working toward the loop.

3 Keep the twine bound closely together and work with an even tension. Do not bind over the top of the loop. When the section of binding is long enough, pass the end of the twine that you have been working with through the loop.

4 With one hand, pull the other end of the twine, making the loop smaller and smaller, until it pulls the end of the twine that you were binding with down under the binding. Trim the ends.

KNOTS AND STITCHES
Crown Sennit

This type of knot can be made from between three and six lengths of string. Once formed, a knot, or "crown," can be linked to another and so on to build up a "sennit." This continuous knotted length is strong and can be used for a range of purposes. Successive crowns may be made in alternate directions (anti-clockwise and then clockwise), if desired, to produce a spiral effect. The success of the sennit depends on drawing up the crowns evenly.

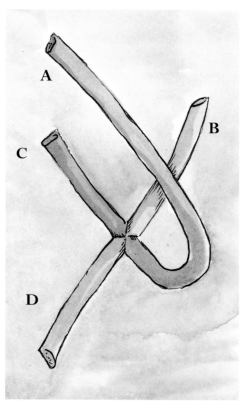

1 To work the knot, take the required number of strings (in this case, four) and whip them together in the center, as shown. Cross string A over string B.

2 Then, cross string B over strings A and C.

3 Next, cross string C over strings B and D.

4 Pass string D over string C and then down through the loop that was formed with string A. Tighten each string gradually to make an even knot. Repeat the process to create the next knot.

Lark's Head Knot

This useful knot, known as a "mounting knot," is often used to mount strings onto a base string, called a "knot anchor," in macramé projects. Any length of string can be used to make the knot, but it must be long enough to pass through the loop.

1 Fold the string in half to make a loop. Hold the loop in front of the "anchor," bend the loop down behind it and then thread through the ends from front to back. Pull the ends to secure the knot.

Flat Knot

This basic knot (also known as a "square knot") is usually worked on a group of four strings that have been knotted onto a "knot anchor" using lark's head knots. Only the outer strings are used to create the knot, so that the inner strings become "knot bearers." Successive knots can be worked in this way to create a neat, strong cord.

1 Attach two looped strings side by side on the "knot anchor" using lark's head knots. Take the right-hand string over the two center strings and then under the left-hand string.

2 Take the left-hand string over the end of this right-hand string, then behind the two center strings and up over the right-hand string.

3 Repeat step 1, working from left to right with the right-hand string.

4 Repeat step 2, working from right to left with the left-hand string. Draw up the ends evenly to secure the knot.

Feather Stitch

This attractive looped stitch is very quick and easy to work, but the stitches must be made evenly to create a neat, regular effect. The stitches are worked on either side of an imaginary central line, and they alternate on either side as the row progresses.

Blanket stitch

This straightforward stitch is most commonly used to finish edges in order to prevent fraying or unraveling, especially on blankets (hence the name). The stitches should be spaced at even intervals, although the "arms" of the stitches can be worked at varying lengths for a decorative finish. Blanket stitch can also be used as a form of decorative knotwork.

1 Make the knot in the string, then bring the bodkin up through from the wrong side of the fabric at A. Insert the bodkin at B and bring it out again at C, passing the string beneath the point of the bodkin before drawing it through. Repeat at even intervals.

1 Make a knot in the string, then bring the bodkin up through from the wrong side of the fabric at A. Insert it at B and bring it out again at C, passing the string beneath the point of the bodkin before drawing it through.

2 Insert the bodkin at D and bring it out again at E, again passing the string beneath the point of the bodkin before drawing it through.

WRAPPED TUMBLERS

THE SIMPLEST APPROACH OFTEN PRODUCES THE MOST PLEASING RESULTS. A BASIC WRAPPING TECHNIQUE IS USED TO COVER THESE TUMBLERS, BUT IT CAN BE DRAMATICALLY VARIED BY USING DIFFERENT WEIGHTS OF STRING. PIPING CORD PRODUCES A SPARE, ELEGANT FINISH, IN CONTRAST TO THE ROUGH-AND-READY APPEAL OF COIR. THE RELEASE TECHNIQUE USED TO WRAP THE GLASSES MAKES THEM PRACTICAL AS WELL AS STYLISH. THE WRAPPING FITS SNUGLY AND IS SECURE AND COMFORTABLE TO HOLD, YET THE GLASS IS EASILY REMOVED FOR WASHING.

1 Turn each tumbler upside down. If it has a dimple in the base or any other shaping that would make release of the finished wrapping difficult, pad out the hollows with clear plastic wrap and thin cardboard. Wrap the entire tumbler in clear plastic wrap.

2 Decide how far up the glass you want to wrap and, using paper towels, cover this area of the plastic wrap with a generous smear of petroleum jelly.

3 Wrap the tumbler in a second layer of clear plastic wrap to cover the petroleum jelly. Tuck the excess plastic wrap inside the tumbler to hold it in place.

4 Starting in the center of the base, apply extra-strong glue to a small area and wind the string in a spiral. Gradually apply more glue as the spiral grows.

5 Continue gluing and wrapping over the edges of the base and up the sides of the tumbler until the desired height is reached.

6 Let dry overnight. Gently twist the tumbler to release the bond between the tumbler and the plastic wrap. Remove the tumbler and peel the remaining plastic wrap from the string wrapping. Cut off the excess string using a scalpel. Apply a coat of matte acrylic varnish to seal and protect the wrapping, if desired.

MATERIALS AND EQUIPMENT YOU WILL NEED

GLASS TUMBLERS • CLEAR PLASTIC WRAP • THIN CARDBOARD (OPTIONAL) • PAPER TOWELS • PETROLEUM JELLY • EXTRA-STRONG WHITE GLUE • GLUE SPREADER • PIPING CORD, COIR OR SISAL • SCALPEL • MATTE ACRYLIC VARNISH (OPTIONAL) • VARNISH BRUSH (OPTIONAL)

STRING-TRIMMED BAG

Carefully appliquéd on a plain linen bag, perfect to hold shoes or lingerie, cotton string takes on a delicate air. The bag could also be appliquéd with a name to make a pretty and practical gift. The coiled ends of the drawstring are both decorative and functional, preventing the string from disappearing into the casing when the bag is opened.

1 Draw around a small, round object on paper to make templates for the dots, and cut them out. The thickness of the string or piping cord will determine the size of the dots. Fold the fabric in half and arrange the templates on one of the fabric rectangles. Pin in place. Avoid placing them too close to the edges.

2 Remove one of the templates and mark its position. Pin the end of a length of string or cord onto the center of the dot. Stitch in place, coiling around and tucking the raw end under as you work.

3 Appliqué all the dots in the same way, then fold under the top edge of each rectangle by ½ inch. Fold over another 1½ inches to make a cuff. Press to mark a guideline. Embroider a row of feather stitches just below the second fold (see Basic Techniques), using three strands of embroidery floss. Unfold the cuff, then pin, baste and machine stitch around the two raw edges of the linen. Leave a small gap near the cuff on one side to allow the drawstring to be inserted.

4 Fold down the cuff. Pin, baste and stitch to form a narrow casing at the bottom of the cuff.

5 Thread string or cord through the casing using a safety pin. Remove the safety pin. Coil each end of the drawstring into a spiral and stitch to secure.

MATERIALS AND EQUIPMENT YOU WILL NEED

PENCIL • SMALL ROUND OBJECT • PAPER • SCISSORS • SOFT WHITE COTTON STRING OR PIPING CORD • 1 PIECE NATURAL-COLORED LINEN FABRIC, 26 X 21 INCHES • DRESSMAKER'S PINS • SEWING NEEDLE • MATCHING SEWING THREAD • IRON • EMBROIDERY NEEDLE • ECRU EMBROIDERY FLOSS • BASTING THREAD • SEWING MACHINE • SAFETY PIN

CLASSIC LAMPSHADES

SIMPLE, CLASSIC SHAPES ARE A TIMELESS ELEGANT CHOICE FOR LAMPSHADES AND BASES. HOWEVER, CLASSIC NEED NOT MEAN DULL. THE LARGER, CONICAL SHADE IS PRODUCED VERY QUICKLY, USING THE OLD SHADE AS A TEMPLATE; IT IS DECORATED WITH SOFT COTTON STRING CURLICUES, WHICH ADD A DELICATE FLOURISH. THE SMALLER SHADE IS A STORE-BOUGHT LAMPSHADE PUNCHED WITH HOLES AND THREADED WITH JUTE TWINE. DECORATIVE PENDANTS OF STRING-WRAPPED BEADS OR MARBLES PROVIDE A WITTY NOTE.

1 For the larger shade, first remove the old lampshade from its frame and flatten out. Place it on top of the lampshade stiffener and draw around the outline with a soft pencil.

2 Cut out the shape with scissors or a craft knife.

3 Turn the shape the other way up. Using a scalpel and a metal ruler, cut a line through the protective film on the lampshade stiffener ½ inch in from one straight edge. Place the watercolor paper on top of the lampshade stiffener. Ease the protective film away from the stiffener, pulling it with a gentle, horizontal rather than diagonal, motion. Smooth the watercolor paper into position with the palm of your hand.

4 Leave the protective film in place on the ½-inch narrow strip that you cut earlier, and finish smoothing the watercolor paper over the lampshade stiffener. Use your thumb to smooth out the paper as you approach the corner.

MATERIALS AND EQUIPMENT YOU WILL NEED

OLD LAMPSHADE • LAMPSHADE STIFFENER • SOFT PENCIL • SCISSORS OR CRAFT KNIFE • SCALPEL • METAL RULER • JAPANESE WATERCOLOR PAPER • SPRAY ADHESIVE • SOFT WHITE COTTON STRING • JUTE TWINE • CLOTHESPINS • INSTANT-BONDING GLUE • STORE-BOUGHT LAMPSHADE • HOLE PUNCH • THREE LARGE BEADS OR MARBLES • TOOTHPICKS • EXTRA-STRONG WHITE GLUE

5 Cut away the excess paper. Use a scalpel and metal ruler to cut the paper along the edge of the narrow strip. Remove the protective film from this strip, form the stiffener into a cone shape and overlap the edges. Press the edges firmly together.

7 For the smaller lampshade, hold one end of the jute twine in a clothespin and twist tightly. Drip instant-bonding glue onto this end to make it neat for threading. Let the glue dry before snipping off the string close to the peg.

9 Starting at the seam of the lampshade, thread the twine through the holes from front to back. Make sure that the tension is relaxed and even.

6 Spray adhesive onto one side of a generous length of string. Allow the string to fall in a swirling pattern onto the lampshade and press gently into place.

8 Using another clothespin as a marker to maintain even spacing, make holes around the base of the store-bought lampshade with a hole punch.

10 When the threading is complete, cut the string and join the two loose ends together using instant-bonding glue.

▶

11 To cover the beads or marbles, cut a generous length of twine and fold it in half to find the center. Using a toothpick, apply extra-strong white glue around the center of each bead or marble and begin wrapping toward one end, applying more glue as it is needed. Then wrap the other half of the bead or marble in the same way. Cut off one end of twine and leave the other long.

12 Tie a loose, simple knot in the long end of the string and glue it onto the lampshade. Make the other two pendants the same way.

GILDED STRING VASE

THE USE OF GOLD LEAF ADDS A NOTE OF GLAMOUR AND OPULENCE TO CREATE THIS WONDERFULLY BAROQUE VASE. THE ROUGH, THREE-DIMENSIONAL JUTE TWINE AND THE SHEEN OF THE GOLD LEAF CONTRAST VERY EFFECTIVELY WITH THE SMOOTH, CLEAR GLASS. GOLD LEAF AND METAL LEAF ARE AVAILABLE AT GOOD ART SUPPLY STORES OR BY MAIL ORDER FROM SPECIALTY SUPPLIERS.

1 Wash and dry the vase thoroughly. Draw a wavy line around the top with a chinagraph pencil. Apply glue to one side of the jute twine, blotting off any excess with your finger. Carefully glue the string onto the wavy line, holding each small section in place as it dries. Cut off the string so that the two ends meet exactly. Let dry.

2 Glue and stick another piece of string beside the first. Glue two straight lines of string above and below the wavy line. Repeat for the base of the vase.

3 Measure the distance between the string borders and mark on paper. Draw a scroll shape between the two marks, leaving a gap of 1/2 inch at each end. Tape the paper inside the vase. Lightly draw over the scroll onto the glass. Remove the template.

4 Glue string onto the scroll. Glue a second piece of string beside the first. Repeat on the opposite side of the vase, then add two more scrolls. Draw wavy lines between the scrolls and cover with string.

5 When the glue is completely dry, paint gilding size onto the string and set aside for 10–15 minutes, until tacky. Tear small pieces of gold or metal leaf and place on the string. Press down firmly, then gently brush with a fine, dry paintbrush. Gild a small area at a time.

6 Gently brush off some of the gold or metal leaf with a wire brush to produce a distressed look. Rub over the gilded string with a clean fingertip to smooth it out. Clean any excess glue from the vase with a damp cloth or scrape it off with a craft knife.

MATERIALS AND EQUIPMENT YOU WILL NEED

VASE • CHINAGRAPH PENCIL • EXTRA-STRONG WHITE GLUE • JUTE TWINE • SCISSORS • RULER • PAPER • PENCIL • MASKING TAPE • GILDING SIZE • GOLD LEAF OR DUTCH METAL LEAF • PAINTBRUSH • WIRE BRUSH • CLOTH OR CRAFT KNIFE

PAINTING AND STAMPING WITH STRING

STRING OFFERS MANY EXCITING POSSIBILITIES AS A PAINTING TOOL. COILED AND GLUED ONTO A BLOCK, IT BECOMES A STAMP THAT MAY BE USED TO ANY SCALE. A TINY STRING SPIRAL DIPPED IN PAINT TURNS PLAIN BROWN PAPER INTO PRETTY GIFT-WRAP AND ADDS GLAMOUR TO A HUMBLE POT. A LARGE COIL OF ROPE PROVIDES AN EXCITING MOTIF FOR DECORATING A PLAIN WALL. WRAPPED AROUND A PAINT ROLLER, STRING PRODUCES RANDOM, WAVY LINES ON GIFT-WRAP THAT ARE REFLECTED IN THE PAPER STRING USED TO TIE THE PACKAGES.

1 To make your own stamps, use a glue gun to stick small spirals of string onto small pieces of wood to make stamping blocks. Let the glue set. When gluing small areas, be careful not to burn your fingers on the glue.

2 Thread the pot onto a length of sash cord to make the pot easier to paint. Apply a base coat of latex or acrylic paint.

3 When the base coat is dry, apply stamping paint onto one of the spiral stamps using a flat brush.

▶

MATERIALS AND EQUIPMENT YOU WILL NEED

GLUE GUN AND GLUE STICKS • WHITE COTTON STRING • SMALL SCRAPS OF WOOD • POT • SHORT LENGTH OF SASH CORD •
LATEX OR ACRYLIC PAINT • FAST-DRYING STAMPING PAINT • FLAT PAINTBRUSHES • PAPER TOWELS • PAINT ROLLER AND TRAY • CRAFT KNIFE •
CARDBOARD TUBE • BROWN WRAPPING PAPER

4 Stamp a few times on paper towels to remove the excess paint, then stamp onto the pot. If you are stamping with different-colored paints, use a different stamp for each color. Let dry.

6 Using the glue gun, attach one end of a length of string to the cardboard tube. Wrap the string around the tube in an open spiral. Cut off the string and glue the loose end inside the tube.

8 Pour some latex or acrylic paint into the paint tray and run the roller through it. Remove the excess paint by rolling on paper towels.

5 To cover a larger area, a paint roller is ideal. Using a craft knife, cut the cardboard tube to fit the paint roller.

7 Slip the cardboard tube over the paint roller, and glue it in place.

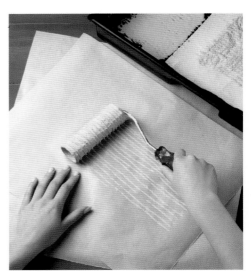

9 Roll the design onto the brown paper, pushing the roller with a smooth, consistent action. Let dry.

CORD-TRIMMED CUSHION COVERS

S ET OFF SIMPLE, EVERYDAY FABRICS WITH WHITE COTTON PIPING CORD AND BRASS EYELETS FOR AN ELEGANTLY MODERN LOOK. THE PLAIN COTTON CUSHION HAS A LOOPED CORD EDGING AND IS FINISHED WITH A DECORATIVE TASSEL AT EACH CORNER. THE CHECKED CUSHION, MADE OUT OF A HUMBLE DISH CLOTH, HAS CORD LACED ACROSS THE BACK AND STURDY KNOTS AT THE CORNERS.

1 Using a ruler and felt-tipped marker, draw a 21-inch square and a 21 x 14-inch rectangle onto the graph paper. Cut out both shapes and pin onto the cotton fabric. Cut one square and two rectangles.

2 Place the square of fabric right side down on a flat surface. Using the dressmaker's pencil, draw a line around the square 1 inch in from the edge. Make marks at 3-inch intervals along each line, starting in each corner. Using the eyelet punch and hammer, punch a hole through the fabric at each mark. Position the eyelet pieces on either side of the holes and hit firmly with the hammer.

3 Fold in ¹/₂ inch along one long edge of each rectangular piece of fabric. Fold in another ¹/₂ inch and iron. Pin, baste and stitch the hems. Mark a line on the wrong side of the fabric around the three raw edges, 1 inch in from the edge. Make marks at 3-inch intervals along each line, starting in each corner. Punch holes in the fabric as before and hammer the eyelets in place. ▶

MATERIALS AND EQUIPMENT YOU WILL NEED

RULER • FELT-TIPPED MARKER• GRAPH PAPER • SCISSORS • DRESSMAKER'S PINS • COTTON FABRIC • DRESSMAKER'S PENCIL • TAPE MEASURE • EYELET PUNCH • HAMMER • BRASS EYELETS • IRON • SEWING NEEDLE • BASTING THREAD • MATCHING THREAD • SEWING MACHINE • CARDBOARD • WHITE COTTON PIPING CORD • FINE WHITE COTTON STRING • 4 BEADS • 2 CUSHION PADS • CHECKED DISH CLOTH

4 Lay the square piece of fabric face up. Place a rectangular piece over it, right sides together, lining up the raw edges. Do the same with the second rectangular piece, so the two hemmed edges overlap. Pin, baste and stitch a seam all the way around. Clip the corners, turn the cushion right side out and iron.

5 Cut two pieces of cardboard 3 x 5 inches and place one on top of the other. Wrap the piping cord seven times around the 3-inch depth of the cardboard, starting and ending at one edge.

Thread a piece of fine string between the rectangles, pull it up to the top and tie in a secure knot. Cut through the piping cord at the opposite end. Unravel the cord and put a bead inside the tassel beneath the knot at the top. Arrange the frayed cord to completely conceal the bead. Bring the two ends of string from the tie down among the frayed cords.

Wrap another piece of string four times around the tassel and tie in a secure knot. Trim the ends of the tassel. Make three more tassels and hand stitch one to each corner of the cushion cover.

6 Insert a cushion pad. Cut a piece of cord approximately five times the width of the cushion and thread it through the eyelets. Tie the two ends neatly together at the back of the cushion.

7 Cut two more rectangles of cotton fabric using the paper pattern piece cut in Step 1. Trim the dish cloth to measure 20 x 28 inches. Mark a center line across the shorter width of the dish cloth with pins. Make a fold 3 inches from the center line on either side, with each fold facing the center. Iron, then baste along each fold 1/2 inch from the edge.

8 Mark the positions of the eyelets with the dressmaker's pencil. Punch holes with the eyelet punch through the two layers of fabric along each fold. Hammer the eyelets in place.

9 Hem one edge of the two rectangular pieces as before. Position them on the dish cloth piece and pin, baste and stitch together. Clip the corners, turn right side out and iron. Mark the position for an eyelet in each corner. Punch holes and hammer the eyelets in place. Insert a cushion pad. Knot a short piece of cord through the eyelet in each corner and knot the ends of the cord to finish. Lace piping cord through the eyelets across the center of the cover as shown.

TWINE-DECORATED FURNITURE

TRANSFORM A DULL OR SHABBY PIECE OF FURNITURE BY MAKING IT SPROUT GREEN LEAVES! THE LEAVES ARE, APPROPRIATELY ENOUGH, MADE FROM GARDEN TWINE, USING TWO SHADES OF GREEN FOR A THREE-DIMENSIONAL LOOK. THE SURFACE IS TREATED FIRST WITH GREEN WOOD DYE, WHICH HAS THE ADDED ADVANTAGE OF DISGUISING SCRATCHES OR WEAR AND TEAR. TRY THIS SIMPLE TECHNIQUE ON A HALL TABLE, A BED OR IN A CHILD'S PLAYROOM FOR A WITTY, EYE-CATCHING EFFECT THAT WILL CERTAINLY NOT GO UNNOTICED.

1 Prepare the surface of the chest of drawers by sanding lightly to remove any wax or sheen.

2 Rub with apple-green wood dye to give a subtle veil of color. Paint the drawer handles with forest-green gouache. Add touches of black, white and brown to give depth. Let dry and seal with a coat of quick-drying acrylic varnish.

3 Tape the drawers securely shut. Apply glue to the pedestal, then wrap forest-green twine around the pedestal in even, parallel rows. Draw a trailing leaf design lightly onto the top of the chest with a pencil. Carefully paint glue over a small section of the design.

4 Apply the forest-green twine over the glue. Pinch the ends of the leaves to give a defined shape. Continue gluing and applying string to small sections of the design until it is complete.

5 Apply leaf-green twine in a curving pattern over the forest-green twine on the pedestal. Let dry thoroughly.

6 Remove the adhesive tape from the drawers. Using a craft knife, cut through the pieces of twine at the points where they prevent the drawers from opening.

MATERIALS AND EQUIPMENT YOU WILL NEED

SMALL CHEST OF DRAWERS • SANDPAPER • APPLE-GREEN WATER-BASED WOOD DYE • PAPER TOWELS OR SOFT CLOTH • PLASTIC GLOVES •
GOUACHE PAINTS: FOREST-GREEN, BLACK, ZINC-WHITE AND BROWN • FINE PAINTBRUSH • QUICK-DRYING ACRYLIC VARNISH • VARNISH BRUSH •
ADHESIVE TAPE • PENCIL • EXTRA-STRONG WHITE GLUE • GLUE BRUSH • GARDEN TWINE: FOREST-GREEN AND LEAF-GREEN • CRAFT KNIFE

BOTTLE CARRIER

PERFECT FOR TRANSPORTING BOTTLES IN STYLE, BE IT HOME FROM THE SUPERMARKET OR TO A SUMMER PICNIC, THIS INGENIOUS CARRIER HOLDS UP TO FOUR BOTTLES SECURELY IN PLACE. THIS PROJECT IS AN IDEAL OPPORTUNITY TO PRACTICE SOME BASIC KNOTS. THE HANDLE IS WORKED IN TWO DIFFERENT KNOTS, BOTH SHOWN IN BASIC TECHNIQUES. THE REST OF THE BOTTLE CARRIER IS COILED AND STITCHED WITH WAXED TWINE, MAKING IT VERY STRONG.

1 For the handle, cut two 12-inch lengths of rope and lay them side by side on a flat surface. Lay a 10-foot length on one side of these two pieces and another 10-foot length on the other side, matching the centers of all four lengths. Start to work a flat knot (see Basic Techniques).

2 Work another flat knot but this time in the opposite direction. The alternating knots will make an interesting pattern.

3 Continue working flat knots until the short lengths of rope are almost used up. Fold the handle in half. Work a crown sennit knot with the remaining four long lengths of rope (see Basic Techniques). ▶

MATERIALS AND EQUIPMENT YOU WILL NEED

FLAX ROPE, APPROXIMATELY 28 YARDS • TAPE MEASURE • CRAFT KNIFE • BLACK WAXED TWINE • LARGE SEWING NEEDLE •
MASKING TAPE • CURVED SEWING NEEDLE • UNWAXED TWINE

4 Continue working crown sennit knots to make a handle of the required length.

5 For the basket, start coiling the remaining length of rope around the base of the handle. Sew the coil together as you work with black waxed twine and a large needle. When the coil is two or three thicknesses of rope wide, remove it from the handle.

6 Continue producing a coil, securing the rope in place with diagonal stitches that go around two thicknesses of rope at a time. When the coil is large enough to hold four bottles, square off the shape, leaving a gap at each corner, and start working up the sides. Keep the tension even and check frequently that the bottles will fit. The rope will tend to work its way inward, so keep the rope loose and the twine tight.

7 Work up the sides and, when they are the required height, cut off the rope at an angle with a craft knife. Wrap the end in masking tape to prevent it from unraveling.

8 Push the handle down through the hole in the bottom of the carrier. Spread each rope at the end of the handle into its individual strands and sew onto the base of the carrier using a curved needle and unwaxed twine.

PICTURE FRAME

THERE IS SOMETHING VERY SATISFYING ABOUT PRODUCING USEFUL AND ATTRACTIVE ITEMS FROM INAUSPICIOUS MATERIALS, PARTICULARLY WHEN THE FINISHED OBJECT IS SOMETHING THAT WOULD BE COSTLY TO PURCHASE READY-MADE. ALL YOU NEED TO MAKE THIS WRAPPED FRAME IS JUTE TWINE AND A PIECE OF CARDBOARD. A COLLECTION OF THESE PICTURE FRAMES, MADE IN VARYING SIZES TO HOUSE A COLLECTION OF RELATED PICTURES OR FOUND OBJECTS, WOULD LOOK STUNNING DISPLAYED TOGETHER.

1 Decide what size you want your frame to be; draw the dimensions onto the mounting board or cardboard using a set square and ruler. To find the center, draw diagonal lines from corner to corner. Then draw the "window" for the front of the picture frame.

2 Cut out the "window" center of the frame using a craft knife and a cutting mat underneath to protect your work surface. In the interests of safety and accuracy, do not attempt to cut through the entire thickness of the board at once; instead make several shallow cuts.

3 Cut a length of jute twine. Short lengths of twine are easiest to work with. Apply glue to a small section of the frame and wrap with the twine. Wrap the string closely together for an even finish. ▶

MATERIALS AND EQUIPMENT YOU WILL NEED

MOUNTING BOARD OR OTHER STURDY CARDBOARD • PENCIL • SET SQUARE • RULER • CRAFT KNIFE • CUTTING MAT • JUTE TWINE • SCISSORS •
EXTRA-STRONG WHITE GLUE • GLUE SPREADER

4   When you reach the end of the first piece of twine, tie on a new length of twine at the back with a simple knot. Apply more glue as you work around the frame.

6   Wrap a piece of twine diagonally across the center of each corner. Wrap first one half of the corner and then the other until it is covered.

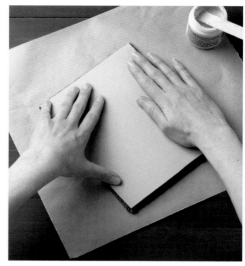

8   Cut a piece of mounting board or cardboard slightly smaller than the wrapped frame and glue it onto the back.

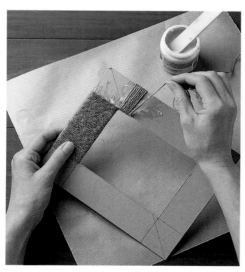

5   When you reach a corner, turn the frame 90° and continue along the next side of the frame, leaving the corner unwrapped.

7   Cut off any loose ends of the twine at the back of the frame, then glue down.

9   Cut a stand from mounting board or cardboard. Mark its position on the back of the frame and glue in place.

WRAPPED CANDELABRA

COILS OF JUTE TWINE APPEAR ALMOST MIRACULOUSLY SUSPENDED BENEATH THE ARMS OF THIS WRAPPED CANDELABRA — EARTHY COUNTERPARTS OF BAROQUE GLASS DROPS. EVEN WITH THE CANDLES EXTINGUISHED, THE CANDELABRA RETAINS A STATELY, MAJESTIC AIR. IN THE INTEREST OF SAFETY, BE CAREFUL NOT TO LET CANDLES BURN RIGHT DOWN TO THE HOLDERS, AND NEVER LEAVE CANDLES UNATTENDED.

1 Turn the candelabra upside down. Glue the end of the twine firmly to one candle holder. Wind the twine around the holder, pushing each line close up to the previous one. When you reach the base, cut off the twine and glue in place. Wrap all the candle holders the same way.

2 Turn the candelabra right way up. Wrap the base with twine, applying the glue gradually. Continue up to the arms.

3 Apply glue to the candelabra stem between the arms. Zigzag the twine from left to right and back again, using the point of a pencil to hold each fold in the twine. Press down firmly or clip in place until dry. Pull the twine over the arm and zigzag it on the next side between the arms, then on the other sides.

4 Continue wrapping the stem above the arms up to the top. Apply glue to one of the arms and wrap, starting on the inside and working toward the end. Wrap each arm in this way.

5 Cut a length of the thicker twine and glue along one side. Carefully roll into a 1 1/2-inch coil, applying more glue as necessary. Make four of these coils and glue one to the underside of each arm on the candelabra.

6 Apply glue around the top of each candle holder and wrap with the thicker twine to cover the rim. Apply glue to the base of each candle holder and wrap the thicker twine around twice.

MATERIALS AND EQUIPMENT YOU WILL NEED
CANDELABRA • EXTRA-STRONG WHITE GLUE • GLUE SPREADER • FINE JUTE TWINE • SCISSORS • PENCIL • THICKER JUTE TWINE

BLANKET DECORATION

THE SOFT, SUBTLE COLORS AND TEXTURE OF WOOL BLANKETS COMBINE BEAUTIFULLY WITH THE NATURAL TONES AND TEXTURE OF STRING AND ROPE. INSTEAD OF THROWING AWAY OLD, FRAYED BLANKETS, TRANSFORM THEM INTO COSY, STYLISH THROWS FOR YOUR LIVING ROOM.

BLANKETS WITH WORN EDGES CAN EASILY BE FRINGED OR NEATENED WITH BLANKET STITCH, USING SOFT WHITE COTTON STRING. ANOTHER STRIKING IDEA IS TO APPLIQUÉ STRANDS OF SISAL ROPE ONTO A BLANKET, LETTING THE STRANDS FALL NATURALLY.

1 For the blanket stitch border, start by machine stitching new hems at each end, if necessary, using matching thread. Turn under the hemmed ends of the blanket. Thread a bodkin or large-eyed darning needle with the cotton string and secure on the back of the blanket with a knot concealed within the first hem. Bring the needle through to the front of the fabric. Work the border in blanket stitch (see Basic Techniques), taking care to keep the tension even. Finish with a knot concealed within the hem.

2 For the appliquéd blanket, cut off the ends of the blanket and fringe the edges by gently removing some of the threads, using a needle. Carefully separate the strands of the sisal rope.

3 Place the blanket on a flat surface and lay a single strand of rope on top, letting it fall naturally in a smooth, curving design. Hold the rope in position with safety pins, then secure with small hand stitches, using a natural-colored thread. Appliqué two more strands of rope in the same way.

MATERIALS AND EQUIPMENT YOU WILL NEED

2 WOOL BLANKETS • SEWING MACHINE (OPTIONAL) • MATCHING MACHINE SEWING THREAD (OPTIONAL) • BODKIN OR LARGE-EYED DARNING NEEDLE • SOFT WHITE COTTON STRING • SEWING NEEDLE • ROUGH-TEXTURED SISAL ROPE • SAFETY PINS • NATURAL-COLORED SEWING THREAD

SEWING BASKET

THE BASIC COILING AND STITCHING TECHNIQUE USED TO MAKE THIS BASKET CAN BE ADAPTED TO PRODUCE A WHOLE RANGE OF BASKETS TO SUIT A VARIETY OF APPLICATIONS. YOU CAN VARY THE WEIGHT OF STRING OR ROPE USED, DEPENDING ON THE SIZE OF BASKET YOU WISH TO MAKE. THICK ROPE, LIKE THE ROPE USED IN THIS PROJECT, GIVES PLEASINGLY QUICK RESULTS; ALTERNATIVELY, YOU CAN USE THIN STRING OR TWINE TO MAKE CHARMING MINIATURE BASKETS FOR HOLDING DRESSING TABLE ITEMS OR JEWELRY.

1 To start the base, coil the end of the rope tightly in your hands.

2 Thread a large needle with the red waxed twine and begin to sew the coil together as you work.

3 Continue producing a coil to form the base of the basket, securing the rope in place with random diagonal stitches that go around two thicknesses of rope at a time. The red twine stitches make an effective contrast pattern against the white rope.

4 When the base is of the required size, start working up the sides. Keep the tension even throughout. The rope will tend to work its way inward, so keep the rope loose and the twine tight. When the sides are the required height, cut off the rope at an angle with a craft knife. Wrap the cut end in masking tape to prevent it from unraveling.

▶

MATERIALS AND EQUIPMENT YOU WILL NEED
WHITE POLYESTER EIGHT-STRAND ROPE, APPROXIMATELY 22 YARDS • LARGE NEEDLE • RED WAXED TWINE • CRAFT KNIFE • MASKING TAPE •
WHITE COTTON FABRIC • SCISSORS • DRESSMAKER'S PINS • SEWING NEEDLE • WHITE SEWING THREAD

5   For the handle, fold a short length of rope in half. Bind the red twine around the loop and whip to secure (see Basic Techniques).

7   Stitch the coil together with the red twine in the same way as the base and sides of the basket.

9   Make the lid slightly larger than the base so it will fit comfortably on top, then work the sides, and finish in the same way as for the base.

6   For the lid, start coiling the end of another piece of rope around the base of the whipped handle.

8   Stitch the loose ends of the handle securely in place on the underside of the lid.

10   Cut a circle of fabric to fit inside the basket plus a ³⁄₄-inch seam allowance. Turn under the raw edge twice and pin around the inside rim of the basket, pleating the excess into even folds. Stitch neatly in place. You can line the lid in the same way, if desired.

KNOTTED DECKCHAIR COVER

THE COMPLEX APPEARANCE OF THIS WONDERFULLY TACTILE DECKCHAIR COVER BELIES THE SIMPLICITY OF THE KNOTTING INVOLVED. ONLY THE MOST ELEMENTARY KNOTS ARE USED, AND THE DESIGN IS WORKED IN CHUNKY SASH CORD TO PRODUCE GRATIFYINGLY SPEEDY RESULTS. THE DESIGN IS SHOWN HERE IN DETAIL ON A CHILD'S DECKCHAIR, BUT THE INSTRUCTIONS APPLY EQUALLY TO AN ADULT SIZE DECKCHAIR. AS WELL AS BEING STRONG AND HARDWEARING, THE JUTE COVER IS ALSO EXTREMELY COMFORTABLE TO SIT ON.

1 Remove the existing cover from the deckchair by taking out the staples with pliers and a screwdriver. Stand the deckchair frame on a flat surface so the bottom seat rail is at the top and at a comfortable working height. Measure the existing cover and cut lengths of the sash cord eight times this length using a craft knife.

2 Fold each length of cord in half. Attach cords from left to right along the bottom rail using lark's head knots (see Basic Techniques). Leave the tails of the knots hanging down. Make sure the rail is completely covered and that the total number of hanging tails is divisible by four.

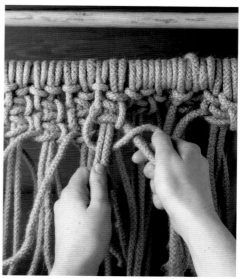

3 Starting from the left-hand side of the rail, work flat knots (see Basic Techniques) on groups of four hanging tails all the way across to the right-hand side. Repeat to form a second row of flat knots, again working from left to right. ▶

MATERIALS AND EQUIPMENT YOU WILL NEED
DECKCHAIR • PLIERS • SCREWDRIVER • UNWAXED JUTE SASH CORD • CRAFT KNIFE

4 Setting aside the first two cords, work flat knots on groups of four cords from the left to the right. Set aside the last two cords.

6 Pass the loose end of this cord beneath the second cord and through the loop. Pull to secure, forming a chained half-hitch knot.

8 Repeat steps 3–7, until the cover is of the required length to fit the deckchair.

5 Holding the second cord from the left taut, bring the first cord out to the left to form a loop that passes over the second cord, as shown.

7 Make another chained half-hitch knot directly below the first, but this time passing the first cord under rather than over the second cord. Repeat steps 5–7, this time using the two loose cords on the right-hand side.

9 Tie the tails securely to the top rail of the deckchair using simple knots. Cover the top rail completely by wrapping two out of each group of four cords twice around the rail before tying off.

PAINTED WALL DECORATION

THE POSSIBILITIES AFFORDED BY THIS UNUSUAL BUT REFRESHINGLY SIMPLE DECORATIVE TECHNIQUE ARE LIMITED ONLY BY YOUR IMAGINATION AND THE TIME AVAILABLE. VERY DETAILED OR COMPLEX DESIGNS CAN BE WORKED ON LARGE AREAS, USING VARIED WEIGHTS OF CORD OR ROPE TO PROVIDE EXTRA TEXTURAL INTEREST. ALTERNATIVELY, YOU COULD RUN A SIMPLE CORD OR ROPE BORDER IN AN UNDULATING WAVE DESIGN AROUND THE TOP OF A BATHROOM WALL TO REINFORCE A NAUTICAL OR SEASIDE DECOR.

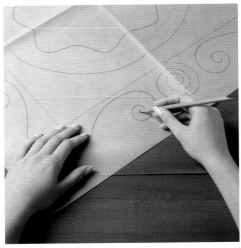

1 On the left-hand side of a large piece of tracing paper, draw half of the design. Attach two pieces of tracing paper with masking tape if necessary. Use a ruler and set square to ensure that the straight lines and angles are accurate. Fold the paper in half and trace over the design onto the right-hand side of the paper. Open the paper out and fold in half the other way to check that the design is symmetrical.

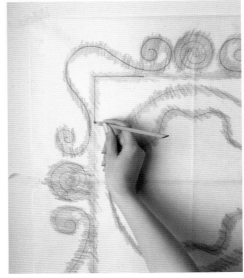

2 Turn the tracing over and rub over the back of the design using the side of the pencil point. Stick the back of the tracing to the wall you wish to decorate, with masking tape. Using a sharp pencil so you can easily see your progress, draw firmly over the lines of the design. This will transfer it to the wall. Remove the tracing paper.

3 Apply glue along the pencil lines on the wall, working in small sections. Stick on the piping cord, wrapping the raw ends with adhesive tape to prevent them from unraveling.

4 When the glue is completely dry, paint over the whole design in the same color as the wall, dabbing around the string and into the corners to ensure good coverage. Let dry, then touch up any areas where the string still shows through.

MATERIALS AND EQUIPMENT YOU WILL NEED

TRACING PAPER • SOFT PENCIL • MASKING TAPE • RULER • SET SQUARE • SHARP COLORED PENCIL • EXTRA-STRONG WHITE GLUE • GLUE BRUSH • PIPING CORD • ADHESIVE TAPE • LATEX PAINT • DECORATOR'S PAINTBRUSH

ROPE-WRAPPED CHAIR

WRAPPED IN SISAL ROPE, A BATTERED OLD JUNK SHOP CHAIR NOT ONLY ACQUIRES A NEW LEASE OF LIFE AS A BEAUTIFUL PIECE OF FURNITURE BUT BECOMES AN OBJECT OF ALMOST SCULPTURAL IMPACT. IT DOESN'T MATTER HOW DAMAGED THE SURFACE OF THE CHAIR IS, AS IT WILL BE COMPLETELY COVERED BY THE ROPE, BUT TRY TO FIND ONE THAT HAS A PLEASING BASIC SHAPE. OLD-FASHIONED WOODEN KITCHEN CHAIRS OR WINDSOR CHAIRS WOULD BE VERY SUITABLE. COMPLETE THE EFFECT WITH A PLAIN CALICO CUSHION.

1 Prepare the chair by cleaning and sanding it to remove any paint or varnish that will prevent the glue from adhering. Repair any major damage with wood filler to provide a smooth, even surface. Let dry thoroughly, then sand off any excess.

2 Wrap the rope around the back rail of the chair, gluing it securely in place. Glue lengths of rope across the back of the seat of the chair and cut them off at the back uprights using a craft knife and cutting mat. Glue lengths of rope across the front of the seat, following the curve carefully. Cut short lengths of rope to glue onto the back uprights next to the back rail.

3 Cut a few short lengths of rope, each one slightly shorter than the next. Glue the short lengths of rope in place to form a triangle on the upright at each side of the back rail (see step 7).

MATERIALS AND EQUIPMENT YOU WILL NEED
NICELY SHAPED WOODEN CHAIR • SANDPAPER • WOOD FILLER • SISAL ROPE • EXTRA-STRONG WHITE GLUE • GLUE SPREADER • CRAFT KNIFE • CUTTING MAT • LARGE CLIPS

4 Wrap the brace between the legs of the chair, adding triangles of rope at the intersections, as before. Begin to wrap the arm rail of the chair, working from the seat upwards. Use large clips to hold the rope in place while the glue dries.

6 Holding the rope securely in place with clips while the glue dries, carefully cut off the excess rope.

8 Wrap the legs, making sure that all the intersections have a triangle of short lengths of rope, as before.

5 Add more rope across the front of the seat until the edges are aligned with the rope wrapping the arm rail.

7 Glue another length of rope across the back of the seat, just in front of the uprights.

9 Wrap and glue rope around the top rail of the chair. Bring the rope down the arm rail and glue in place. Make sure the rope is exactly in line with the arm of the chair. ▶

10 Wrap and glue an additional length of rope around the front of each arm to conceal any raw edges.

12 Glue a length of rope across the center of the seat from the back to the front, holding the end with a clip. Trim to length. Add more lengths of rope on either side of this first length to completely cover the seat.

11 Holding the end securely in a clip, glue rope diagonally over the seam between the top rail and each back upright. Overwrap any other seams that need to be either concealed or embellished.

FRINGED SHELF EDGING

THE SIMPLEST AND MOST INEXPENSIVE OF SHELVES ASSUMES DESIGNER STATUS WHEN ADORNED WITH A FRIVOLOUS SKIRT OF RAFFIA. YOU CAN ADAPT THE TECHNIQUE TO SUIT DEEPER SHELVING, EITHER BY BRAIDING WITH MORE STRANDS OF RAFFIA OR BY USING THICK ROPE INSTEAD. IF YOU ARE USING ROPE, FRAY THE ENDS TO PRODUCE THE FRINGED EFFECT. YOU CAN TRIM THE ENDS OR LEAVE THEM IRREGULAR FOR A NATURAL LOOK.

1 Bunch together 60 strands of raffia about one-and-a-half times as long as the shelf to be edged. Attach one end to a door handle or nail using a rubber band.

3 To produce a flat braid, keep your thumbs on top, as turning your thumbs toward the center would produce a round cord.

5 Pull the loose ends through the loop to form a lark's head knot (see Basic Techniques). Add bunches of raffia along the whole length of the braid in the same way. Trim the ends to make an even fringe if desired.

2 Divide the raffia into three groups of 20 strands and begin to braid evenly.

4 Cut some shorter pieces of raffia and group them in bunches of ten. Fold the first group of ten in half to form a loop. Push this loop through one of the loops in the braid.

6 Finally, attach the shelf edging to the shelf using drawing pins or double-sided tape.

MATERIALS AND EQUIPMENT YOU WILL NEED
RAFFIA • SHELF • LARGE RUBBER BAND • SCISSORS • DRAWING PINS OR DOUBLE-SIDED TAPE

FOOD COVER

STORE-BOUGHT FOOD COVERS ARE ALL TOO OFTEN GARISH STRUCTURES OF BRIGHTLY COLORED PLASTIC SUPPORTING A LAYER OF UNATTRACTIVE NYLON MESH. IN THIS VERY DIFFERENT COVER, FABRIC STIFFENER TURNS ORDINARY WHITE COTTON STRING INTO A SCULPTURAL MATERIAL THAT WILL RETAIN THE MOST UNEXPECTED SHAPES INDEFINITELY. SHORT LENGTHS OF JUTE TWINE, SIMPLY KNOTTED AND FRAYED, ADD A PRETTY DECORATION OF WISPY BUTTERFLIES TO COMPLETE THIS VERY UNUSUAL KITCHEN ACCESSORY.

1 Place the flour sifter lid or other small, dome-shaped item on the base of an upturned plastic bowl. Pad out the shape with clear plastic wrap to make the mold for the food cover, and secure with adhesive tape. Cover the whole mold in plastic wrap to produce a smooth surface.

2 Smear the mold with petroleum jelly and cover with another layer of plastic wrap.

3 Pour the fabric stiffener into a large bowl. Cut a generous length of string. Wearing plastic gloves, place the string into the bowl and squeeze the liquid into the string until the string is saturated with fabric stiffener. ▶

MATERIALS AND EQUIPMENT YOU WILL NEED

LID OF FLOUR SIFTER OR SIMILAR SMALL, DOME-SHAPED ITEM • PLASTIC BOWL • CLEAR PLASTIC WRAP • ADHESIVE TAPE • PETROLEUM JELLY • FABRIC STIFFENER • LARGE BOWL • WHITE COTTON STRING • SCISSORS • PLASTIC GLOVES • JUTE TWINE • EXTRA-STRONG WHITE GLUE • GLUE SPREADER

4 Lay lengths of string in evenly spaced parallel lines over the mold, starting in the center and working down each side. Cut off each length, leaving some overhanging the edge. The weight of these long ends will help form a neat finished shape. Continue until the mold is covered.

5 Again starting in the center, lay a second layer of string lengths on top of the first, in the opposite direction. Space and trim this layer as before.

6 Wrap a length of saturated string three times around the base of the mold to form a firm rim. Twist two short lengths of saturated string together to make a handle. Form into a circle and attach to the top of the structure, tucking the ends neatly into the layers of string. Let dry overnight.

7 When completely dry, gently twist the food cover to release the surface tension and remove from the mold.

8 Twist a short length of jute twine around the handle and glue in place with extra-strong white glue, neatly tucking in the raw ends.

9 Tie short lengths of jute twine in simple knots randomly over the surface of the food cover. Fray the ends to make decorative "butterflies."

NATURAL CURTAIN

HUNG WITH NATURAL KEEPSAKES COLLECTED DURING EXPEDITIONS TO THE SEASHORE AND COUNTRYSIDE, THIS SIMPLE STRANDED CURTAIN IS A KIND OF "LIVING SCRAPBOOK." NEW OBJECTS CAN BE ADDED AS THEY ARE ACQUIRED, AND THE SLIGHTLY ROUGH TEXTURE OF THE JUTE TWINE HOLDS EACH OBJECT PERFECTLY IN PLACE. A FALLEN BRANCH MAKES THE IDEAL SUPPORT. AMBER, STRAY FEATHERS, EVEN HUMBLE TWIGS AND BOTTLE CAPS ALL ASSUME TALISMANIC IMPORTANCE WHEN DISPLAYED WITH SUCH ADMIRABLE RESTRAINT.

1 Cut the branch to fit the width of your window and secure at a comfortable working height by hanging with twine. Cut lengths of jute twine twice the required height of the curtain. Fold each length of twine in half and pass the folded end over the branch from front to back.

2 Pass the ends of each length of twine through the loop and pull tight, forming a lark's head knot (see Basic Techniques). Attach the lengths of twine along the branch in this way at equal intervals.

3 Hold the beads and various found objects up against the lengths of twine to begin planning your design. Drill a hole in the objects if necessary. ▶

MATERIALS AND EQUIPMENT YOU WILL NEED

BRANCH • HAIRY JUTE TWINE • SCISSORS • SELECTION OF FOUND OBJECTS: LEAVES, BEADS, SHELLS, CRUSHED BOTTLE CAPS, TWIGS, SEMI-PRECIOUS STONES, ETC. • DRILL (OPTIONAL) • INSTANT-BONDING GLUE

4 Apply a few drops of instant-bonding glue to the end of each piece of twine and let dry, to make threading easier.

5 Thread one of the collection of objects onto the twine and tie a knot below it to hold it in place.

6 Thread a second object onto the next piece of twine, but at a slightly different height.

7 Vary the design by attaching some items with a reverse lark's head knot. Fold the twine to form a loop at the point at which you want to attach the object. Push the loop through the hole in the object and pass the remaining length of twine through the loop.

8 Vary the planes in which the objects lie by making two holes in suitable objects, such as bottle caps. Thread the twine through one of the holes from the back to the front. Now thread the twine back through the other hole so the bottle cap or other object lies flat against the twine.

9 Take care to pull the twine very gently through fragile objects such as dried leaves or feathers.

NAUTICAL LIGHT PULL

THIS OUTSIZE LIGHT PULL REPLACES THE WHITE NYLON LIGHT PULLS, THAT SO EASILY BECOME GRUBBY, FOUND IN SO MANY HOMES. CORD TIED WITH A FEW SIMPLE KNOTS GIVES IT A JAUNTY NAUTICAL APPEARANCE THAT YOU CAN EXTEND AS A THEME FOR DECORATING THE WHOLE BATHROOM. THE CHUNKY KNOTS AND BEADS GIVE A PLEASING CONTRAST OF TEXTURE EVERY TIME YOU SWITCH THE LIGHT ON OR OFF. YOU COULD ALSO MAKE A BLIND PULL IN THE SAME WAY, USING NATURAL-COLORED CORD AND WOODEN BEADS.

1 Fold the cord in half and pinch together to mark the center point.

2 Use one half of the cord to form three blanket stitches around the other half of the cord, working along from the center (see Basic Techniques).

4 Glue the red beads between the loops as decoration. Alternatively, stitch the beads in place with matching sewing thread.

To fit the light pull, unscrew and remove the existing light pull, leaving the part attached to the ceiling still in place. Bring the two ends of the sash cord up around the part of the light pull that is attached to the ceiling. Using matching or contrasting twine, whip securely in place around the remaining part of the light pull, concealing it within the whipping (see Basic Techniques).

3 Glue the halves of the cord together along their length, leaving the last 2 inches free. Hold them together with clips while the glue dries.

MATERIALS AND EQUIPMENT YOU WILL NEED
RED-AND-WHITE SASH CORD, 7 FEET LONG • EXTRA-STRONG WHITE GLUE • GLUE SPREADER • LARGE CLIPS • RED BEADS • SEWING NEEDLE AND MATCHING THREAD (OPTIONAL) • MATCHING OR CONTRASTING TWINE

STRING-APPLIQUÉD CURTAINS

ORDINARY WHITE COTTON STRING IS EXCELLENT FOR LARGE-SCALE FURNISHING PROJECTS SUCH AS THESE FULL-LENGTH CURTAINS. THE APPEALING, CHILD-LIKE DESIGN OF LARGE DAISIES IS APPLIQUÉD DIRECTLY ONTO THE PLAIN BACKGROUND FABRIC. FOR A CHILD'S ROOM YOU COULD STITCH THE WHITE FLOWERS ONTO A BRIGHT-COLORED FABRIC. COMPLETE THE WINDOW DECORATION WITH THESE SPLENDID TASSELED CURTAIN POLE FINIALS — FEW PEOPLE WILL REALIZE THAT THEY ARE, IN FACT, MADE FROM TWO OLD-FASHIONED FLOOR MOPS!

1 Decide on the size of the finished curtains. Add 2 inches to the width and 3½ inches to the length and cut the curtains from the linen or linen-like fabric. Fold in ½ inch along the long sides of the fabric and iron. Fold over another ⅝ inch. Pin, baste and stitch the hems, then iron.

2 Measure the width of the curtains and decide how many tabs are needed, assuming that the tabs will be 2¾ inches wide with 3½-inch gaps between them. Multiply the number of tabs by 9½ inches; cut a strip of fabric to this length and 6½ inches wide. Fold the strip of fabric in half lengthwise. Pin, baste and stitch along the long edge with right sides together, leaving a ½-inch seam allowance.

3 Press the seams open. Turn the tubes the right way out and iron flat with the seam positioned centrally on one side of the tube. Cut the strip into 9½-inch lengths. Tuck a foldover of ½ inch at each end inside the tab. Pin, baste and stitch in place.

▶

MATERIALS AND EQUIPMENT YOU WILL NEED

LINEN OR LINEN-LIKE FABRIC • TAPE MEASURE • SCISSORS • IRON • DRESSMAKER'S PINS • SEWING NEEDLE • BASTING THREAD • MATCHING THREAD • SEWING MACHINE (OPTIONAL) • DRESSMAKER'S PENCIL • WHITE COTTON STRING • WHITE SEWING THREAD • 2 MOP HEADS • SCRAP PAPER • MASKING TAPE • COPPER PAINT • PAINTBRUSH • 2 METAL BRACKETS TO FIT DIAMETER OF POLE • COPPER POLE TO FIT THE WINDOW • GLUE GUN AND GLUE STICKS

4 Fold in ½ inch along the top edge of the curtains and iron. Fold over another 1¼ inch. Pin, baste and stitch the hems. Fold the tabs in half and pin onto the curtains, leaving 3½-inch gaps between them. Line up the bottom of the tabs with the bottom of the hem. Baste and stitch in place. Fold in ½ inch along the bottom of the curtains and then another 1½ inches. Pin, baste and stitch the bottom hems.

6 Tuck the end of the white cotton string over the top of the curtain. Stitch securely in place with a needle and white thread. Pin the string along the marked line, approximately 12 inches at a time or up to a floral motif marker. Hand stitch in place using tiny slip stitches.

8 Cover the string on the mop heads with scrap paper to protect it. Stick a piece of masking tape around the metal top. Paint the wooden part with copper paint and let dry.

5 Lay the curtains right side up on a flat surface. Measure lines from the top to the bottom of the curtains approximately 18 inches apart. Mark with pins, then draw the lines with a dressmaker's pencil. Decide on the positions of the floral motifs, approximately 24 inches apart, and mark with pins.

7 To sew a floral motif, loop the string to form a petal shape and pin in place. Stitch the petal to the fabric. Repeat until the flower has six petals. Continue stitching the string down the marked pencil line to the bottom of the curtain. When the string appliqué is complete, carefully iron the curtains.

9 Paint the metal brackets with copper paint. When dry, thread the curtain tabs onto the copper pole and thread a bracket on to each end. Glue the mop head finials on to each end of the pole using a glue gun. (The glue can be snapped off when the curtains need laundering and reapplied when they are re-hung.) Attach the brackets to the wall above the window.

GREETING CARD

INEXPENSIVE SCRAPS OF PAPER TAKE ON A SOPHISTICATED AIR WHEN DELICATELY BOUND TOGETHER BY A LENGTH OF JUTE STRING TO FORM A UNIQUE HANDMADE CARD. STRANDS PULLED FROM A PIECE OF PLASTERER'S SCRIM WILL GIVE YOU LENGTHS OF JUTE OF SUITABLE FINENESS. THE SIMPLE CUT-OUT OAK LEAF MOTIF PROVIDES A PERFECTLY MATCHED GIFT TAG. IF YOU SCENT THE OIL USED TO MAKE THE PAPER TRANSLUCENT, THIS WILL GIVE THE CARD A REALLY SPECIAL EXTRA-SENSORY DIMENSION.

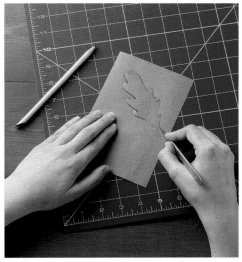

1 Scent some olive oil with a little essential oil, if desired. Working on a protected surface, use paper towels to rub the olive oil over a sheet of calligraphy paper until it becomes translucent. Let dry.

2 Cut a piece of green sugar paper to form the front of the card. Draw an oak leaf shape approximately one-third of the way down from the top.

3 Cut out the leaf shape with a craft knife on a cutting mat. Set the leaf shape aside.

▶

MATERIALS AND EQUIPMENT YOU WILL NEED

OLIVE OIL • ESSENTIAL OIL (OPTIONAL) • PAPER TOWELS • CALLIGRAPHY PAPER • GREEN SUGAR PAPER • SCISSORS • PENCIL • CRAFT KNIFE • CUTTING MAT • PAPER GLUE • WATERCOLOR PAPER • METAL RULER • EXTRA-STRONG WHITE GLUE • BODKIN • FINE JUTE TWINE OR PLASTERER'S JUTE SCRIM

4 Glue the oiled paper on top of the sugar paper. The oil will cause uneven sticking, which gives the finished card an attractive mottled appearance. Set aside, until completely dry, under a pile of books. Protect the books with several layers of paper towels to absorb any residual oil.

6 Cut the oiled paper to the same size as the green paper. Apply glue to the top two-thirds of the torn side of the folded watercolor paper. Glue the layered green paper and oiled paper in place to form the front of the greeting card.

8 Cut a piece of green paper and a piece of oiled paper to the width of the greeting card, about half the height of the gap left below the oiled and green paper. Tear across the top edges. Glue the green paper to the inside of the card along the bottom and glue the oiled paper to the torn edge.

5 Score down the center of the watercolor paper using the back of a craft knife and a metal ruler, and fold to make the greeting card. Tear away most of the paper on one side of the fold to produce a deckled edge.

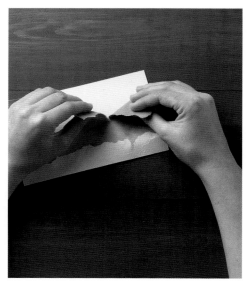

7 Tear across the front of the greeting card just below where the glue ends, and remove the bottom third.

9 Make holes in the front of the card with a bodkin and thread through the twine to join the upper and lower parts. Tie a simple knot at each end of the string.

For the gift tag, make a hole in the cut-out leaf shape. Attach a length of string to the leaf using a lark's head knot (see Basic Techniques). Carefully score a central, curving vein along the leaf using the back of the craft knife.

KEY CUPBOARD

THE SECRET OF PERFECT STORAGE IS ACCESSIBILITY AND VISIBILITY, ALLOWING INSTANT RETRIEVAL OF STORED OBJECTS. REPLACING THE SOLID FRONT OF THIS WOODEN CUPBOARD WITH A SINGLE LENGTH OF THREADED TWINE MEANS THAT YOU WILL NOT BE IN ANY DOUBT AS TO THE WHEREABOUTS OF THE KEY TO THE LIQUOR CABINET. ATTACH NAILS TO THE BACK OF THE CUPBOARD FOR HANGING THE KEYS. THE CUPBOARD WOULD ALSO BE A USEFUL PLACE TO KEEP JEWELRY OR OTHER VALUABLES BEAUTIFULLY DISPLAYED.

1 Cut into the rebate on the back of the cupboard door using a scalpel and metal ruler. In the interests of safety and accuracy, do not attempt to cut through the entire thickness of the wood at once; instead make several shallow cuts. Remove the solid door panel.

2 Measure and note the dimensions of the rebate.

3 Cut strips of soft wood to make the four sides of a simple frame that will fit snugly into the rebate. Hold the two shorter pieces together with masking tape. Drill a row of evenly spaced ⅛-inch holes through both pieces simultaneously.

4 Glue the four sides of the frame together with a glue gun, making sure that the holes along the top and bottom of the frame are facing each other.

5 Thread the jute twine through the holes from top to bottom in one continuous length, maintaining an even tension. Secure the twine with a simple knot at each end.

6 Glue the string screen into the rebate. Cut lengths of masking tape to cover the seam.

MATERIALS AND EQUIPMENT YOU WILL NEED

SMALL WOODEN KEY CUPBOARD • SCALPEL • METAL RULER • PENCIL AND PAPER • STRIPS OF SOFT WOOD • MASKING TAPE • DRILL AND WOOD BIT • GLUE GUN AND GLUE STICKS • JUTE TWINE

WOVEN STOOL SEAT

MANY HOMES HAVE AT LEAST ONE RUSH STOOL OR CHAIR SEAT THAT WOULD BENEFIT FROM RENOVATION BUT IS NOT WORTH THE EXPENSE OF PROFESSIONAL ATTENTION. RUSH OR SEAGRASS IS NOT ALWAYS READILY AVAILABLE TODAY, AND THE NOTION OF LEARNING WHAT SEEMS TO BE A SPECIALIZED CRAFT CAN BE A LITTLE DAUNTING. INSTEAD, THIS SIMPLE WEAVING TECHNIQUE ALLOWS YOU TO USE ROPE FOR THE SEAT, TO GREAT PRACTICAL AND VISUAL EFFECT. THE LARGE, BLUNT WOODEN AWL IS A VERY USEFUL TOOL FOR THIS PROJECT.

1 Divide the rope into three bundles for ease of handling. Mark each cut and bind in each place with masking tape to stop the ends from fraying when you cut. Choose a screw that is long enough to go through the end of the rope and into the wood of the stool but without coming out on the other side. Screw through the end of one of the rope bundles and into the center of the first strut (strut A), on the inside of the stool.

2 Pull the rope parallel with strut A and take it over the second strut (strut B).

3 Take the rope all the way around strut B and then back over strut A, as shown. Maintain an even tension on the rope as you work.

MATERIALS AND EQUIPMENT YOU WILL NEED
¼-INCH UNBLEACHED COTTON ROPE, APPROXIMATELY 39 YARDS • CRAFT KNIFE • MASKING TAPE • 2 WOOD SCREWS •
RUSH STOOL WITH SEAT REMOVED • SCREWDRIVER • LARGE NEEDLE • TWINE OR STRONG THREAD • LARGE WOODEN AWL

4 Bring the rope up through the middle of the stool and over the third strut (strut C).

6 Using twine or strong thread, stitch the end of the rope securely to the adjacent piece of rope.

8 When the short sides of the stool are complete, work the middle of the stool in a figure of eight, adding more rope as necessary.

5 Continue working around the stool in this way, passing the rope over and around each consecutive strut, until you reach the end of the first bundle.

7 Wrap the end of the next bundle of rope with masking tape and stitch it in place so that it butts up to the end of the first bundle.

9 The weaving will become tighter and more difficult to work as you fill the center. Use a large awl to create as much space as possible until no more rope can be fitted in.

▶

10 Finish off the loose end of the last bundle of rope by stitching it as in step 6. Tuck the end neatly inside the weaving.

11 Finally, use the awl to flatten out and neaten up any irregularities in the weaving.

NAPKIN RING

THIS DELIGHTFULLY SIMPLE EXAMPLE OF STRINGWORK IS MADE USING TWO DIFFERENT KINDS OF STRING LOOSELY TWISTED TOGETHER AND TREATED AS ONE STRAND. SOFT WHITE COTTON STRING COMBINES BEAUTIFULLY WITH THE NATURAL COLOR AND HARSHER TEXTURE OF JUTE TWINE TO GIVE AN IRRESISTIBLY TACTILE RESULT. A SET OF MATCHING NAPKIN RINGS WOULD LOOK WONDERFULLY ELEGANT WITH PLAIN LINEN NAPKINS OR A DAMASK TABLECLOTH. THE RING IS WORKED ENTIRELY IN BLANKET STITCH.

1 Cut a length of cotton string and a length of jute twine both four times the circumference of the finished napkin ring. Twist the two loosely together.

3 Complete the circle and cut off any excess.

5 When you have completed the circle, cut off the loose ends and glue in place. Tuck in the raw ends neatly.

2 Form the two into a circle. Wrap one end around and through the circle several times to make a secure ring.

4 Using the remaining long end, work in blanket stitch around the circle (see Basic Techniques).

MATERIALS AND EQUIPMENT YOU WILL NEED
SOFT WHITE COTTON STRING • JUTE TWINE • SCISSORS • EXTRA-STRONG WHITE GLUE • GLUE SPREADER

BEADED PITCHER COVER

Assorted beads serve as decoration and also to weight down this pitcher cover, which is made in moments from a scrap of plasterer's scrim. Plasterer's scrim is an open-weave fabric used to attach plasterwork layers and is readily available at hardware and specialty craft stores. The cover is a stylish modern version of the traditional milk pitcher cover and is reminiscent of summer meals outdoors. This is a lovely way to use a collection of beautiful old glass beads.

1 Drape the scrim over the pitcher to ascertain the required finished size.

3 Gently remove a few weft threads from each cut edge by hand to produce a fringe.

5 At each corner, thread a bead onto one of the double-warp threads at the edge of the scrim, then tie the two threads in a double knot around the bead.

2 Cut the scrim to the required length. Take care to cut between the weft (horizontal) threads as this will give a neat edge.

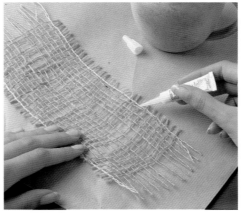

4 Drip glue along the long edges of the scrim, where the warp and weft threads cross, to strengthen the edge.

6 Thread beads onto the loose warp threads at each end of the scrim, tying a simple knot to secure each bead in place. Tie the knot at a different point on each thread to produce an attractive undulating edge.

MATERIALS AND EQUIPMENT YOU WILL NEED

PITCHER • SMALL PIECE OF PLASTERER'S JUTE SCRIM • SCISSORS • INSTANT-BONDING GLUE • ASSORTED GLASS BEADS

TWINE TASSEL

THIS GENEROUSLY SIZED TASSEL, WITH ITS SKIRT OF GREEN GARDEN TWINE, WOULD MAKE AN IMPOSING ADDITION TO A CURTAIN TIE-BACK, OR WOULD PROVIDE SPLENDOR AS A TRADITIONAL KEY TASSEL. WORKED OVER A CURTAIN POLE FINIAL, THE TASSEL USES THE SIMPLEST OF PASSEMENTERIE TECHNIQUES TO STUNNING EFFECT. THE STRIPED CORD IS MADE USING TWO DIFFERENT COLORS OF TWINE, TWISTED TIGHTLY TOGETHER IN THE CHUCK OF A HAND DRILL FOR A REALLY PROFESSIONAL EFFECT.

1 To make the cord, wind the brown twine 12 times around two immobile objects 4 feet apart. Wind the thinner green twine approximately 40 times around the same two objects until it is the same thickness as the bundle of brown twine. Knot the two colors together. Secure a cup hook in the chuck of a hand drill. Loop the twines over the cup hook at one end and over a clamp or door handle at the other.

2 Turn the drill handle clockwise to twist the twine until it is so tightly spun that it is about to kink.

3 Without loosening the tension of the twisted twines, release the end that is attached to the clamp or door handle, and carefully loop it around the clamp and attach it to the cup hook, alongside the first end.

▶

MATERIALS AND EQUIPMENT YOU WILL NEED

THICK BROWN AND FINE GREEN GARDEN TWINE • SCISSORS • CUP HOOK • HAND DRILL • CLAMP (OPTIONAL) • DRILL WITH WOOD BIT • CURTAIN POLE FINIAL • THICK KNITTING NEEDLE • INSTANT-BONDING GLUE • GLUE SPREADER • MOUNTING BOARD OR WOOD, 8 x 11 INCHES

4 Turn the drill handle counter-clockwise to twist the two colors together, producing a tight cord. Bind both ends of the cord tightly to prevent them from unraveling.

6 Wind green twine 50 times around the 11-inch length of the piece of mounting board or wood. Tie the loose ends together. Pass a short piece of twine through one end of the loop and tie off firmly. Remove the tied loop from the board. Repeat to make a total of ten loops.

8 Apply glue liberally to the top of the skirt. Remove the knitting needle from the finial, then thread the cord through the hole in the finial and pull it up so that the top of the skirt sits inside the finial. Cut through the looped bottom end of the skirt. Finally, trim the tassel to an even length.

5 Drill a 1/2-inch hole through the finial from top to bottom. Insert a thick knitting needle through the hole and apply glue liberally to the top half of the finial. Wind brown twine around the finial over the glue, starting from the top. Apply more glue and continue winding until the finial is completely covered with twine. Rotate the finial on the knitting needle to avoid overhandling so that the work remains clean.

7 Using the short piece of twine, tie each loop onto the end of the twisted cord, spacing them evenly to form the skirt of the tassel.

ACKNOWLEDGMENTS

String and rope are widely available internationally at hardware stores, craft stores, department stores, garden-supply stores and garden centers.

The publishers would like to thank the following craftspeople for making projects in this book: Emma Hardy for the gilded string vase, cord-trimmed cushion covers, wrapped candelabra, painted wall decoration and string-appliquéd curtain; Penny Boylan for the string-trimmed bag; Tessa Brown for the bottle carrier, sewing basket and the woven stool seat; and Anna Crutchely for the tassel.

They would also like to thank those people who kindly lent items for the gallery: Knots and Pots, Tallowater, Braddock, Lostwithiel, Cornwall PL22 0RH (01208 872271) for the dice cup and bell rope; Marjorie Self (c/o the Publishers) for the appliquéd cowboy; Paperchase, Tottenham Court Road, London, for the twine-wrapped candlestick; Lakeland Plastics, Alexandra Buildings, Windermere, Cumbria LA23 1BQ for the string bag and the wine cooler; V.V. Rouleaux, 10 Symons Street, London SW3 2TJ (0171 730 4413) for the tassels; The India Shop, 5 Hilliers Yard, Marlborough, Wiltshire SN8 1NB (01672 515585 for

mail-order details and branches) for the child's hanging chair, and the Conran Shop, Fulham Road, London SW3 6RD (0171 589 7401) for the turned string holder.

The following shops kindly supplied items for this book and may be useful sources of a range of additional items: The Bead Shop, 43 Neal Street, Covent Garden, London WC2H 7PJ (0171 240 0931); Berol (products available at arts-and-crafts stores, and stationers), suppliers of pencils used throughout; Bostik (0116 251 0015 for stockists), suppliers of instant-bonding glue, as well as glue guns and glue sticks; Brats, 281 King's Road, London SW3 5EW (0171 351 7674), suppliers of "Mediterranean palette" colors used; Copperstones, 105 High Street, Marlborough, Wiltshire SN8 1LT (01672 515074), suppliers of the tumblers; Country Gardens (01635 873700), suppliers of the child's deckchair; Crucial Trading (0171 221 9000 for stockists), suppliers of natural flooring; The Dollshouse Draper, Lightcliffe, Halifax, Yorkshire HX3 8RN (01422 201275 for mail-order details), suppliers of silk ribbons; The English Stamp Company, Sunnydown, Worth Matravers, Dorset BH19 3JP (01929 439117 for stockists and

mail-order details), suppliers of stamping paints and applicators; The Faerie Shop, 22 Hughenden Yard, Marlborough, Wiltshire SN8 1LT (01672 515995), suppliers of additional beads; Liberon (01797 367555 for stockists), suppliers of water-based wood dye used on the twine-decorated chest of drawers; 3M Adhesives (available at arts-and-crafts stores, and stationers), suppliers of spray adhesive; The Natural Fabric Company, Wessex Place, 127 High Street, Hungerford, Wiltshire RG17 0DL (01488 684002), stockists of a diverse range of high-quality natural fabrics; Paint Magic, 116 Sheen Road, Richmond, Surrey SW9 1UR (0181 940 5503), suppliers of special-effect paints; Panduro (mail-order in the UK, outlets in Scandinavia, 0181 847 6161 for catalogs), suppliers of the fabric stiffener; Specialist Crafts Ltd, PO Box 247, Leicester LE1 9QS (0116 251 0405 for mail-order details), suppliers of lampshade stiffener and stockists of a huge range of craft supplies; Eliza Tinsley, supplier of rope for the wrapped chair; The White Company (0171 385 7988 for mail-order details), suppliers of elegant and useful textiles. Thanks to Faber & Faber for supplying a reference copy of *The Ashley Book of Knots*.

AUTHOR'S ACKNOWLEDGMENTS

Special thanks to Peter Williams, for his elegant photography and to Joanna Lorenz for giving me the opportunity to write this book. Thanks to all those who contributed to this book, whether by loaning items for photography or by making designs. Finally, thanks to Andrew and Daisy for supporting me during the production of this book.

INDEX